MW01138975

Reference to

Grammar

Sharon Sorenson

Also by Amsco:
A QUICK REFERENCE TO THE RESEARCH PAPER
A QUICK REFERENCE TO STUDY AND TEST-TAKING SKILLS

AMSCO

AMSCO SCHOOL PUBLICATIONS, INC.
315 Hudson Street
New York, NY 10013

Artwork by: Hadel Studio

Text and Cover Design: Merrill Haber

Compositor: Northeastern Graphics Services, Inc.

Please visit our Web site at: www.amscopub.com

When ordering this book, please specify:
either **R 723 P** or
A QUICK REFERENCE TO GRAMMAR

      ISBN 978-1-56765-083-9
      NYC Item 1-56765-083-8

Printed in the United States of America

2 3 4 5 6 7 8 9 10   15 14 13 12 11 10 09 08 07

Contents

To the Student

This Quick Reference book differs from other grammar books. It cuts directly to the point and puts what you need to know into simple terms, charts, and other visuals. You probably didn't know grammar could be so simple!

Part 1
Parts of Speech

All the words in the English language are labeled according to how they work in a sentence. We call these labels *parts of speech*. If you can understand only seven parts of speech, you'll know what you need to know about grammar.

The seven parts of speech you need to know are as follows:

noun
pronoun
adjective
verb
adverb
preposition
conjunction

We'll show you, without fancy words, how to figure them out.

 **ALL ABOUT NOUNS**

A noun names a person, place, or thing. **A noun can name one thing, two or more things, or show ownership.**

1

Nouns That Name One Thing	Nouns That Name Two or More Things	Nouns That Show Ownership
a computer	two computers	a computer's hard drive
one disk	a dozen disks	three disks' contents
the printer	several printers	the printer's ink cartridge

General and Exact Nouns

Most nouns name general things. Other nouns name exact things.

General Names	Exact Names
computer	IBM ThinkPad
car	Ford Taurus
television	Sony
park	Central Park

Notice that nouns that name exact things begin with a capital letter.

TIP: To strengthen your writing, use exact names whenever possible.

Activity: Look around you. Make a list of the people, places, or things you see. Then make a second list beside the first in which you change as many general names as you can to exact names.

EXAMPLES:

General Names	Exact Names
man	Mr. Henry
street	Park Avenue

Some nouns also name a group, like the nouns *class* or *team*. We'll talk more about them later.

Using Nouns

Here's what you need to know about nouns to speak and write well:

1.   Add -*s* or -*es* to most nouns to make them name more than one thing. Nouns that name more than one thing are called *plural* nouns. Compare these nouns and their plurals:

Singular Nouns	Plural Nouns With -*s*
a sport	two sports
the rocket	several rockets
a cloud	some clouds
my truck	three trucks
your memo	many memos

Singular Nouns	Plural Nouns With *-es*
a brush	four brushes
the dish	these dishes
my watch	our watches
this church	these churches
one tomato	a dozen tomatoes

2. Some nouns have odd plurals. Compare these nouns:

Singular Nouns	Odd Plurals
a knife	three knives
one goose	a flock of geese
the child	several children
one foot	two feet

If you're unsure about a plural word, check your dictionary. If the word has an odd plural, the dictionary will list it beside the abbreviation *pl.*, which stands for *plural.*

3. Use an apostrophe to make a noun show ownership. While *computers* is plural (more than one), *computer's* with the apostrophe shows ownership, as in *a computer's hard drive.* The hard drive belongs to the computer.

Here are the simple ways to use apostrophes to show ownership:

Ownership With Singular Nouns

Make singular nouns possessive by adding '*s*, like this:

Singular Nouns	Singular Possessive Nouns
a hamburger	a hamburger's flavor
one umbrella	one umbrella's colors
the subway	the subway's schedule

Ownership With Plural Nouns

Make plural nouns that do not end in -*s* possessive by adding '*s*, like this:

Plural Nouns	Plural Possessive Nouns
three children	three children's boots
four men	four men's stories
two mice	two mice's nests

Make plural nouns that end in -*s* possessive by adding an apostrophe at the end.

Plural Nouns	Plural Possessive Nouns
two candles	two candles' flames
all the pots	all the pots' covers
five teams	five teams' uniforms

Comparing Plurals With Possessives

Compare these plural nouns with the possessive ones:

Singular	Singular Possessive	Plural	Plural Possessive
a car	a car's engine	two cars	two cars' engines
a chair	a chair's legs	two chairs	two chairs' legs
a bush	a bush's leaves	two bushes	two bushes' leaves
a woman	a woman's wig	two women	two women's wigs
a deer	a deer's antlers	two deer	two deer's antlers

TIP: Don't confuse plural words with words that show ownership. Some folks scatter apostrophes through their writing like others salt their french fries. Use the apostrophe to show ownership.

Activity 1:   Think about your school neighborhood. Then make a list like the one above in which you list ten nouns that name people, places, or things in your school neighborhood. Then write the singular possessive, the plural, and the plural possessive.

Activity 2: From the list you created in Activity 1 above, choose one noun from each of the four columns. Then write a sentence using each correctly.

4. Capitalize nouns that name exact things. The general name *park* becomes a specific name in *Central Park*, the name of the exact park. Compare these nouns:

General Nouns	Exact Nouns (Capitalized)
a person	George Washington
a computer	IBM ThinkPad
the software	Microsoft Word
some shoes	Nikes

5. Some nouns refer to a group, and they usually take singular verbs. It may seem illogical to describe a group as singular, but grammar isn't always logical. Still, a group usually acts as a single unit, so perhaps there's some logic to it after all. So, nouns that name a group, like *class* or *jury*, need singular verbs (and we'll talk more about verbs later).

Group Nouns	Verbs
The *class*	*begins* work at 8:00 A.M.
Our football *team*	*was practicing* late.
The *jury*	*is* still out.
The student *cast*	usually *performs* well.
Our *choir*	*is going* on tour.

>>>>>>>>>>>>>> **ALL ABOUT PRONOUNS** <<<<<<<<<<<

A pronoun is a shortcut. It keeps us from having to repeat the same noun over and over. Compare these two sentences:

Using only nouns: *Daryl* takes *Daryl's* book bag with *Daryl* to school every day.

Using nouns and pronouns: *Daryl* takes *his* book bag with *him* to school every day.

People Pronouns

Pronouns that refer to people are the most common pronouns. They are listed here:

	Naming Pronouns	Receiving Pronouns	Owning Pronouns
Speaker(s)	I	me	my, mine
	we	us	our, ours
Person(s) Spoken To	you	you	your, yours
	you	you	your, yours
Person(s) Or Things Spoken About	he, she	him, her	his, her, hers
	it	it	its
	they	them	their, theirs

Study these sentences to see how the pronouns are used in sentences:

We sat in the row behind *them* at the stadium.

They gave *us* *your* tickets by mistake.

Activity: Think about your best friends. Then write three sentences in which you use at least two pronouns each.

Using Pronouns

These six easy hints will help you use pronouns correctly:

1.   The pronoun agrees with the noun it refers to. If the noun is plural (*cell phones*), the pronoun referring to it must be plural (*they*). Compare these nouns and their pronouns:

Singular Nouns	Singular Pronouns
The *driver*	drove *his* car as carefully as *he* could.
Yesterday, *Trina*	played *her* best round of golf. *She* broke par.
The old hunting *dog*	lay with *its* head on *its* paws.

Plural Nouns	Plural Pronouns
The *players*	psyched *themselves* up for the big game.
The *menus*	were neatly stacked in *their* places.
All you *students*	need to clean out *your* lockers.

2.   Avoid apostrophes with possessive pronouns. You use an apostrophe to show ownership with nouns, like *Jason's house* or *the city's buses*. But you do not use an apostrophe to show ownership with pronouns, like *his house* or *its buses*.

Pronouns Take No Apostrophes

ours	his
yours	its
hers	theirs

Compare these nouns and pronouns in their possessive forms:

Possessive Nouns (with apostrophes)	**Possessive Pronouns (with no apostrophes)**
Jason's house	his house
city's buses	its buses
your business	business of yours

TIP: The words *its* and *it's* cause lots of confusion. Here's why:

The word *it's*, with the apostrophe, means "it is." The apostrophe shows that the "i" is missing.

The pronoun *its*, like other pronouns, uses no apostrophe.

Here's a simple way to figure out whether to write "its" or "it's":

Step 1: Substitute "it is" for the word in question.

Step 2: If "it is" makes sense, use the apostrophe to show that the "i" is missing.

Step 3: If "it is" does not make sense, leave out the apostrophe.

Compare these two sentences:

Sentence 1: It's well past noon.

Step 1: It is well past noon.

Step 2: *It is* makes sense.

Step 3: Use the apostrophe to show that the "i" is missing.

Sentence 2: The truck lost its brakes.

Step 1: The truck lost it is brakes.

Step 2: *It is* makes no sense.

Step 3: Omit the apostrophe. (*Its* shows that the brakes belong to the truck.)

Activity: Try to remember a favorite toy from your early childhood. From your recollection, write two sentences using *its* correctly. Then write two sentences using *it's* correctly. Use the steps above to see if you used the words correctly.

3. When a pronoun and a noun are used together, use the pronoun that makes sense by itself. Here's how to think through the problem:

Step 1: Omit the noun.

Step 2: Use the pronoun that makes sense.

Here's how it works:

Problem 1: Us/We students were honored for our attendance.

Step 1: Us/We . . . were honored for our attendance.

Step 2: We . . . were honored for our attendance.

Solution: We students were honored for our attendance.

Problem 2: The school board handed out diplomas to us/we students.

Step 1: The school board handed out diplomas to us/we. . . .

Step 2: The school board handed out diplomas to us.

Solution: The school board handed out diplomas to us students.

Activity: Picture in your mind's eye favorite members of your family. Then write four sentences of your own similar to the ones above in which nouns and pronouns appear side by side. Use the steps above to see if you used the pronouns correctly.

4. When two pronouns are used together, try them one at a time to choose the correct one.

Problem 1: The telephone calls were from he/him and I/me.

Think: The telephone calls were from *him.* The telephone calls were from *me.*

Solution: The telephone calls were from him and me.

Problem 2: The media specialist and she/her and I/me made a joint presentation about our new Web site.

Think: *She* made a presentation.
I made a presentation.

Solution: The media specialist and she and I made a joint presentation about our new Web site.

Activity: Think about someone you admire. Then write two sentences similar to the ones above in which two pronouns are used together. Use the problem-solution steps above to see if your pronouns are correct.

5. Avoid *hisself* or *theirselves*. Only the following pronouns correctly end with "self" or "selves":

myself	ourselves
yourself	yourselves
himself, herself, itself	themselves

6. Make a pronoun agree with its verb and other pronouns. That sounds simple enough, but some pronouns that refer to general people, places, or things are singular; some are plural; and some can be singular or plural.

Let's look first at the pronouns that are always singular:

Singular Pronouns

someone	one	anyone	everyone	either
somebody	no one	anybody	everybody	neither
each	nobody			

TIP: How can you remember which words are singular? Here's an easy trick: Think of these pronouns with the word "single" put in the middle:

every-single-one
some-single-one
any-single-body

Then use the singular verb and singular pronoun:

Everyone is in his seat.
Everyone = singular pronoun (every-single-one)
is   = singular verb
his   = singular pronoun

(See more about singular and plural verbs in the section ALL ABOUT VERBS on page 18.)

Activity: Think about a group to which you belong—at school, at church, or in your neighborhood. Then write four sentences, each using a different pronoun from the above list of pronouns that are always singular. Use the tip above to check if your sentences are correct.

Next, let's look at the four pronouns that are always plural:

Plural Pronouns

---

several   few   both   many

If you think about it, each of these four pronouns is logically plural since all four of them always refer to more than one person, place, or thing:

Several of the glasses were broken.

A *few* of the cartons are leaking.

Both of the girls have won awards.

Many of our teammates are first-class athletes.

Finally, let's look at five pronouns that can be singular or plural:

Singular and Plural Pronouns

---

some   any   all   none   most

TIP: If the pronoun can be singular or plural, how do you know whether to use a singular or plural verb? It's easy. Just look at the word nearest the verb for agreement. For example:

Pronoun	Word Nearest the Verb	Verb
Some	of the *neighbors*	*enjoy* the monthly block parties.
Some	of the *water*	*leaks* out every day.
All	of the *apples*	*were* in storage.
All	of the *flour*	*is* in storage.

Activity 1: In your mind's eye, picture a grocery or market in your neighborhood. Write two sentences using the pronoun *some*. In one sentence make *some* singular; in the other sentence make *some* plural.

Activity 2: Write two sentences using the pronoun *most*. In one sentence make *most* singular; in the other sentence make *most* plural.

 ALL ABOUT ADJECTIVES

An adjective describes a noun or pronoun and tells *what kind, which one,* or *how many.*

What Kind	Which One	How Many
a *kind* person	the *tall* person	*one* person
a *shaggy* dog	the *flop-eared* dog	*five* dogs
a *sports* car	the *red* car	a *dozen* cars

Using Adjectives

Adjectives are easy, so there's only one hint to help you use them correctly:

Use clues to show how one thing compares with another. Most adjectives use the endings *-er* and *-est* as clues to show how one thing compares to another. For instance:

Describing one girl:
Shawna is *kind.*

Comparing two girls:
Shawna is *kinder* than Diedre.

Comparing three or more girls:
    Shawna is the *kindest* of the four girls.

If the adjective is long, use *more* instead of *-er* and *most* instead of *-est*. For example:

Describing one race:
    The dirt-bike race was *spectacular*.

Comparing two races:
    Yesterday's dirt-bike race was *more spectacular* than today's.

Comparing three or more races:
    Maybe tomorrow's dirt-bike race will be the *most spectacular* we've ever seen.

TIP: Avoid using *-er* or *-est* along with *more* or *most*. Compare these sentences:

Incorrect: Kelly runs more faster than Gerald.

Correct: Kelly runs faster than Gerald.

Activity 1:   Think about the players on an athletic team in your school. Then write three sentences in which you compare two items using *more* or *-er* endings with the adjectives.

Activity 2:   Rewrite the three sentences you wrote above so that they compare three or more items using *most* or *-est* endings with the adjectives.

>>>>>>>>>>>>   **ALL ABOUT VERBS**   <<<<<<<<<<<<

A verb shows action or state of being. The action is usually easy to identify. Compare these examples:

Action Verbs	State of Being Verbs
walk	is
drive	was
fly	feel
speak	are

Singular and Plural Verbs

A verb, like a noun, is singular or plural. But here's the strange part: Unlike a noun, a verb that ends in -s is singular. Look at this sentence:

The clock (singular noun) ticks (singular verb).

Here are some more examples:

Singular Nouns	Singular Verbs
(without an -s)	(with an -s)
personal pager	beeps
door	is locked
cat	meows
microwave oven	works

Plural Nouns (with an -s)	Plural Verbs (without an -s)
personal pagers	beep
doors	are locked
cats	meow
microwave ovens	cook

Activity 1: Think about a place that you enjoy visiting. Then write four sentences with singular nouns and singular verbs.

Activity 2: Rewrite the four sentences above to use plural nouns and plural verbs. What happened to the endings of the nouns and verbs?

Action and Linking Verbs

Most verbs show action.

EXAMPLE: The storm *terrorized* every dog in the neighborhood.
(*Terrorized* is an action verb. It tells what the storm did to the dogs.)

EXAMPLE: Violent wave action *eroded* the beach.
(*Eroded* is an action verb. It tells what the wave action did.)

Other verbs are linking. They link the subject to a word that describes or renames the subject:

EXAMPLE: The storm *was* violent in Daytona Beach.
(The linking verb *was* connects the subject *storm* with *violent*. Notice that *violent* describes the subject *storm*.)

The following are always linking verbs:

is	was	be
am	were	been
are		being

Some verbs can be linking or action:

seem	appear	remain
become	grow	stay

Some are verbs of the senses:

look	smell	taste
sound	feel	

TIP: Action verbs are stronger than linking verbs, so you should use action verbs rather than linking verbs in your writing. As you proofread your writing, look for the words that are always linking and rewrite the sentence to strength the verb, like this:

Weak Linking Verb	Strong Action Verb
The sunshine was hot on my skin.	The sunshine burned my skin.
After football practice, he was tired.	After football practice, he fell asleep from exhaustion.
Since he hadn't eaten all day, Christopher was hungry.	Since he hadn't eaten all day, Christopher gobbled down a sandwich.

Activity 1:   Recall a party or dance you've attended. Write two sentences about the event using action verbs and two sentences using linking verbs.

Activity 2:   Check the two sentences you wrote above using linking verbs. Rewrite them using action verbs.

Using Verbs

The following simple hints will help you use verbs correctly.

1. Use verb tenses to show changes in time, from the present to the past to the distant past and from the present to the future to the far-reaching future. There are three simple tenses: **today, yesterday,** and **tomorrow:**

Today	Yesterday	Tomorrow
I walk.	I walked.	I will walk.
You sing.	You sang.	You will sing.
He thinks.	He thought.	He will think.

TIP: Helping verbs show time or a change in time. Here are the helping verbs:

is	am	are	was	were
have	has	had		
do	does	did		

Notice how the time changes in these four sentences:

Sentence 1:   Christopher and his sister *took* turns yesterday mowing the grass.

Sentence 2:   Until Dad came home, Christopher and his sister *were taking* turns mowing the grass.

Sentence 3:   Before Christopher and his sister worked out a plan, they never *had taken* turns.

Sentence 4:   Now they *are taking* turns without complaining.

The following chart shows how verbs change time.

Today	Yesterday	Before That	Tomorrow	After That
walk	walked	had walked	will walk	will have walked
sing	sang	had sung	will sing	will have sung
think	thought	had thought	will think	will have thought

Activity: Recall a severe storm you witnessed, perhaps involving rain, snow, wind, hail, or a sandstorm. Write four sentences about the storm similar to Sentences 1, 2, 3, and 4 above. Be sure your sentences show a change in time. Underline the words that help you show the change in time.

2.   Use irregular verbs correctly. Some of the more common ones follow (check others in your dictionary):

begin	began	have/has begun
bite	bit	have/has bitten

blow	blew	have/has blown
break	broke	have/has broken
bring	brought	have/has brought
catch	caught	have/has caught
choose	chose	have/has chosen
come	came	have/has come
do	did	have/has done
draw	drew	have/has drawn
drink	drank	have/has drunk
drive	drove	have/has driven
eat	ate	have/has eaten
fall	fell	have/has fallen
fly	flew	have/has flown
freeze	froze	have/has frozen
get	got	have/has got or gotten
give	gave	have/has given
go	went	have/has gone
grow	grew	have/has grown
know	knew	have/has known
lose	lost	have/has lost
ride	rode	have/has ridden
ring	rang	have/has rung
run	ran	have/has run
say	said	have/has said
see	saw	have/has seen
shake	shook	have/has shaken
speak	spoke	have/has spoken
steal	stole	have/has stolen
take	took	have/has taken
tear	tore	have/has torn
throw	threw	have/has thrown
wear	wore	have/has worn
write	wrote	have/has written

>>>>>>>>>>> ALL ABOUT ADVERBS <<<<<<<<<<

An adverb describes a verb, an adjective, or another adverb. It tells when, where, or how.

When: We registered cold temperatures *yesterday.* (*Yesterday* tells "when" about the verb *registered.*)

Where: Austin walked *home.* (*Home* tells "where" about the verb *walked.*)

How: Nikki walked *slowly.* (*Slowly* tells "how" about the verb *walked.*)

Fred's computer will download *extremely* fast. (*Extremely* tells "how" about the adverb *fast.*)

We registered *extremely* cold temperatures. (*Extremely* tells "how" about the adjective *cold.*)

Activity: Recall a visit to an amusement park, carnival, or street fair. Write three sentences about your visit using adverbs. Make at least one adverb describe "when," another tell "where," and the third explain "how." Label each adverb by what it tells.

Using Adverbs

Adverbs, like adjectives, use -*er* or *more* or -*est* or *most* to show comparisons:

Describing one: When she wore her glasses, Katlin saw *clearly.*

Comparing two:	Since she got new glasses, she sees *more clearly*. (compares her vision now with then)
Comparing more:	Now, she sees *most clearly* with her contacts. (compares her vision now with all other times)

TIP: **Avoid using two negative words together.** Avoid combinations like these:

Incorrect:	We don't hardly ever work. (*Don't* and *hardly* are both negative words.)
Correct:	We hardly ever work.
Incorrect:	They don't have no books. (*Don't* and *no* are both negative words.)
Correct:	They have no books.
Correct:	They don't have any books.

Activity: Try to recall a time when you heard two negative words used incorrectly together. Write two correct sentences.

 ALL ABOUT PREPOSITIONS

Prepositions are little words that can cause big trouble, so let's get to the bottom of the problem. A preposition tells how two words in a sentence are connected, as in "the book *on* the shelf" as opposed to "the book *under* the shelf."

See how the prepositions connect *car* and *overpass* and how each preposition changes the meaning in this sentence:

	Preposition	
	across	
	along	
	around	
	behind	
	below	
	beneath	
	beside	
Sara drove her car	beyond	the overpass.
	by	
	down	
	from	
	near	
	onto	
	over	
	through	
	to	
	toward	
	under	

Recognizing Prepositions

Here's an easy way to identify a preposition:

TIP: Think of a preposition as any place a mouse can run:

A mouse can run *above* the doorsill,
> *around* the corner,
> *down* the hall,
> *up* the stairs,
> *across* the threshold,
> *without* effort,
> *until* midnight.

Here is a list of the most common prepositions:

about	at	beyond	from	out
above	before	by	in	over
across	behind	with	into	through
after	below	down	like	to
against	beneath	during	without	toward
along	beside	except	of	under
around	between	for	off	up

Activity: Recall a visit to the doctor or dentist. Write five sentences about your visit. In each sentence, use at least one preposition from the list above.

Prepositional Phrases

A preposition and the word that answers "who" or "what" after it (called the object) and all the words in between make up what we call the prepositional phrase:

Preposition	+	Words in Between	+	Who or What (Object)
in		the screen's upper left		corner
under		the door		frame
past		four traffic		signals

Activity: Look at the five sentences you wrote in the activity
immediately above. Underline the preposition once.
Underline twice the word that answers "who" or "what" after
each preposition.

Using Prepositions

The following details about prepositions will help you
speak and write well:

**1.   Use the correct word to answer "who" or "what"
after a preposition.** When the word that answers "who"
or "what" is a pronoun, sometimes writers and speakers
use the wrong word. For example:

Incorrect: Just *between you and I*, the food tastes
bad.

Correct: Just *between you and me*, the food
tastes bad.

TIP: The pronouns that answer "who" or "what" are listed
below. How can you remember which one to use? It's
easy. Put "to" in front of each of them, and see if it makes
sense.

(to) me   (to) him
(to) us   (to) her
(to) you   (to) it
               (to) them

Activity: Recall a time when you had a disagreement with someone. Write four sentences about the experience. In each sentence use a different pronoun from the list above as the word that answers "who" or "what" after a preposition.

2.   To avoid subject-verb agreement errors, don't let a prepositional phrase affect which verb you use.

Here's an easy way to get the subject-verb agreement right: Omit the prepositional phrase and then check the subject-verb agreement. Like this:

Problem 1:   The bunch of grapes is/are ready to eat.

   Prepositional phrase: The bunch <u>of grapes</u> is/are ready to eat.

   Omit phrase: The bunch . . . is ready to eat.

Solution: The bunch of grapes is ready to eat.

Problem 2:   The autumn trees along the highway add/adds color to the drive.

   Prepositional phrase: The autumn trees <u>along the highway</u> add/adds color to the drive.

   Omit phrase: The autumn trees . . . add color to the drive.

Solution: The autumn trees along the highway add color to the drive.

Activity: Recall a dream you have. Then write three sentences like those in Problems 1 and 2 above and show how you chose the correct verb.

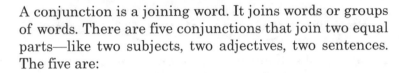

ALL ABOUT CONJUNCTIONS

A conjunction is a joining word. It joins words or groups of words. There are five conjunctions that join two equal parts—like two subjects, two adjectives, two sentences. The five are:

and	nor
but	for
or	

Using Conjunctions

You need to remember two things about conjunctions:

1. When you join two sentences with one of the five conjunctions, use a comma in front of the conjunction.

Like this:

Sentence One	Comma and Conjunction	Sentence Two
The train arrived at the station on time	, but	so many passengers boarded that it left the station late.
The ink-jet printer sits on his desk	, and	the laser printer sits on the shelf above.
The afternoon bus always runs late	, or	I'm always early.

TIP: When you join two sentences, it is incorrect to omit either the comma or the conjunction. Compare these three sentences:

Incorrect: **Missing Comma**
The computer modem seemed to function <u>properly but</u> we knew lightning had struck the system.

Incorrect: **Missing Conjunction**
The computer modem seemed to function <u>properly, we</u> knew lightning had struck the system.

Correct: **Comma and Conjunction**
The computer modem seemed to function <u>properly, but</u> we knew lightning had struck the system.

Activity: Think about the perfect place to live. Write three pairs of sentences about that place. In each pair of sentences, correctly join the pairs with a comma and a conjunction.

2. Don't string sentences together with several conjunctions.

Have you ever heard an excited child tell about an event almost without pausing for a breath? If you string together a whole series of sentences, your writing reads like that child's breathless account. Compare these two passages:

WEAK PASSAGE:

We saw a great movie <u>and</u> then went out for burgers <u>and</u> Cokes <u>and</u> then drove to the arcade <u>and</u> played games until after midnight.

BETTER PASSAGE:

We saw a great <u>movie, and </u>then we went out for burgers and Cokes. After that, we drove to the arcade <u>and</u> played games until after midnight.

Part 2
Sentence Parts

Actually, you can get by knowing very little about parts of a sentence; but the more you understand, the better your sentence will be. Generally, if you can understand only three parts, you'll do just fine. The three parts are:

verb
prepositional phrase
subject

We'll skip the fancy words and explain how you find the three basic sentence parts in three easy-to-do steps. So here we go:

Step 1: Cut out any prepositional phrases.

You remember about prepositional phrases from Part 1? We used the easy trick of finding prepositional phrases by looking for groups of words that tell where a mouse can run.

Because prepositional phrases only add description, they are not part of the basic sentence. So mentally, cross them out, like this:

Sentence: The boxes on the shelf below the
                window held several pairs of boots.

Omit phrases: The boxes . . . held several
                pairs . . .

A mouse can run *on the shelf*; it can run *below the window*.
Of boots is also a prepositional phrase.

Once you cut out the prepositional phrases, see how
few words you have to worry about? You've reduced the
sentence from thirteen words to five!

Step 2:   Find the verb.

With the sentence reduced to only a few words, you're
ready for the next step, finding the verb. You already
know about verbs. A verb is the word that changes time.

Here's a quick, simple two-step way to find the verb:

Step 1:   Add the word "yesterday" or "tomorrow" in
              front of the sentence.

Step 2:   See which word(s) change. That's the verb.

Here's how the steps work:

Sentence: The boxes on the shelf below the
                window held several pairs of boots.

              Step 1:   Yesterday, the boxes . . . held
                        several pairs . . .
                        Tomorrow, the boxes . . . will
                        hold several pairs . . .

              Step 2:   *Held* changed to *will hold*. So
                        the verb is *held*. It's the word
                        that changed time.

Step 3: Find the subject.

Only one final step remains, and here it is: Find the subject. Once you know verb (the word that changes time), finding the subject is easy. Just ask "who" or "what" in front of the verb. The word that answers your question is the subject.

Here's how the step works:

Sentence: The boxes on the shelf under the window held several pairs of boots.

Omit phrases: The boxes . . . held several pairs . . .

Verb: held

Ask: Who or what held?

Answer: boxes

So, *boxes* is the subject of the sentence.

Activity: Write five sentences about whatever you can see out the window. Then follow the three-step plan to find the basic sentence parts: (1) Cut out prepositional phrases, (2) identify the word that changes time (the verb), and (3) find the word that answers "who" or "what" in front of the verb (the subject). Label each.

Part 3
Subject–Verb Agreement

We've just talked about basic sentence parts, particularly the subject and verb. So why is it important to know about subjects and verbs?

The subject and verb of a sentence must agree with each other. That means if the subject is singular (one), then the verb must be singular. If the subject is plural (more than one), then the verb must be plural.

TIP: Remember that most singular nouns do not end in *-s* but singular verbs do:

Singular Nouns (do not end in *-s*)	Singular Verbs (end in *-s*)
A cab *driver*	*honks* his horn regularly.
The *subway*	*offers* the quickest route.
The hotel *lobby*	*looks* a little shabby.

Most plural nouns end in -*s* but plural verbs do not:

Plural Nouns (end in -*s*)	Plural Verbs (do not end in -*s*)
Most cab *drivers*	*honk* their horns regularly.
The *subways*	*offer* the quickest route.
Some hotel *lobbies*	*look* a little shabby.

Reaching Agreement

Here are seven simple ways to make sure your subjects and verbs agree.

1. Make the verb agree with its subject, not with some other word in the sentence.

Incorrect: This jar of pickles taste sweeter than usual.

Correct: This jar of pickles tastes sweeter than usual.

The subject is *jar*, not *pickles*; so, the verb is singular to agree with the singular *jar*.

TIP: One common error in subject-verb agreement is making the verb agree with the object of a preposition instead of the subject. It's an easy error to make.

It's also an easy error to correct. Here's how.

Remember the tip you learned in Part 1 about prepositions being "any place a mouse can run"? And remember the three-step plan for finding sentence parts in Part 2?

Step 1 was to cross out any prepositions and their objects. Now you'll see why those two details are so important.
Let's review:

Problem 1:   The mural on the walls shows/show the town's history.

> **Step 1:**
> **Omit phrase:**   The mural . . . shows the town's history.
>
> **Step 2:**
> **Find verb:**   Yesterday the mural . . . *showed* the town's history.
>
> **Step 3:**
> **Find subject:**   Who or what showed? Answer: mural
>
> **Make verb agree with subject:** mural shows

Solution: The mural on the walls shows the town's history.

Problem 2:   The snacks stored on the lower shelf usually get/gets stale.

> **Step 1:**
> **Omit phrase:**   The snacks stored . . . usually *get* stale.
>
> **Step 2:**
> **Find verb:**   Yesterday, the snacks stored . . . usually *got* stale.
>
> **Step 3:**
> **Find subject:**   Who or what get? Answer: snacks

Make verb agree with subject:
snacks get

Solution: The *snacks* stored on the lower shelf usually *get* stale.

Activity: Recall a park or garden you've visited, read about, or seen on television. Write three sentences about it. In each sentence, include a prepositional phrase between the subject and its verb. Then, using the steps above, check to make sure you've used the correct verb.

2.   The words *here* and *there* can never be subjects.

Incorrect: Here is the three tickets for the concert.

Correct: Here are the three tickets for the concert.

TIP: If a sentence starts with either *here* or *there*, the subject will follow the verb. In the sentence above, the subject is the plural word *tickets*. As a result, the plural subject calls for the plural verb *are*.

Activity: Think about your favorite holiday. Then write two sentences beginning with "Here" and two sentences beginning with "There." Underline the subject in each.

3.   Singular pronouns need a singular verb. You'll remember the singular pronouns we listed earlier:

someone	one	anyone	everyone	either
somebody	no one	anybody	everybody	neither
each	nobody			

Remember to think *some-single-one, any-single-one, every-single-one*. (Review page 14.) These words are singular and take a singular verb. Compare these two sentences:

Incorrect:	Every one of the contestants were nervous.
Correct:	Every one of the contestants was nervous.
Think:	Every-single-one . . . was nervous.

4. Pronouns that can be singular or plural take verbs that agree with the noun nearest the verb. There are only five pronouns that can be singular or plural. They are

some	none
any	most
all	

When you use one of these words, you'll look to the noun nearest the verb to make the verb agree. (Review page 15.) Compare these two sentences:

Incorrect:	None of the envelopes has correct postage.
Correct:	None of the envelopes have correct postage.
Think:	. . . Envelopes have correct postage.

The plural noun *envelopes* calls for a plural verb *have*.

NOTE: This is the only situation where the verb agrees with something other than the subject.

5. When you have singular subjects joined by *and*, use a plural verb.

> Incorrect: The tornado and its accompanying wind was responsible for over $1 million in damages.
>
> Correct: The tornado and its accompanying wind were responsible for over $1 million in damages.
>
> Think: tornado and wind were

In this sentence, *tornado* is joined by *and* with *wind*; together, they form a plural subject.

TIP: Think 1 and 1 = 2.

>   1   and 1   = 2
> The wind and rain   = *scare* us.
> Sunshine and humidity = *make* uncomfortable conditions.
> Our cat   and dog   = *sleep* together.

6. When you join two subjects with *or* or *nor*, make the verb agree with the nearer subject. Compare these two sentences:

> Incorrect: Wind chimes or a hanging flower basket always adorn her patio.
>
> Correct: Wind chimes or a hanging flower basket always adorns her patio.

The verb agrees with the nearer subject, so

> *basket adorns*

If the two subject nouns were reversed, the verb would agree with *chimes*, as in "A hanging flower basket or wind chimes always adorn the patio." Thus,

> *chimes adorn*

TIP: Remember three equations:

    1 or 1 = 1
    1 or 2 = 2
    2 or 1 = 1

Here's how these simple equations look in English:

1	or 1	= 1
The ice cream	or the iced tea	= is enough to cool you!
The bus driver	or the trucker	= was at fault.
1	or 2	= 2
The ice cream	or the iced tea	= are enough to cool you!
The bus driver	or the truckers	= were at fault.
2	or 1	= 1
The iced tea	or the ice cream	= is enough to cool you!
The bus drivers	or the trucker	= was at fault.

Activity: Recall your favorite musicians. Then write three sentences similar to the three patterns above. Make sure the verb agrees with the noun nearest it.

7. Nouns that name groups are usually singular. Compare these two sentences:

Incorrect: The cast of this year's drama production are a great team.

Correct: The cast of this year's drama production is a great team.

Cast takes a singular verb *is* and a singular name *team*.

Part 4
Writing Good
Sentences

Now that you understand all about subjects and verbs, you're ready to get at the nitty-gritty about sentences.

You've no doubt been told that a sentence has a subject and verb and expresses a complete thought. In a nutshell, that's it. But that definition doesn't help much if you've been told you're writing sentence fragments.

 **FRAGMENTS**

A sentence fragment, as the name implies, is a piece of a sentence written as if it were a complete sentence.

Three kinds of fragments crop up in poor writing:

fragments without subjects
fragments without verbs
"baby sentences"

Fragments Without Subjects

Sometimes writers omit subjects, usually because the previous sentence suggests the subject. Compare these sentences:

Sentence: He cashed his paycheck at the bank.

Fragment (no subject):   Then drove home.

Corrected (subject added):   Then he drove home.

Corrected (joined to first sentence): He cashed his paycheck at the bank and then drove home.

Sentence: The new drum major led the marching band during the half-time performance.

Fragment (no subject):   And received wild applause for his efforts.

Corrected (subject added):   And he received wild applause for his efforts.

Corrected (joined to first sentence): The new drum major led the marching band during the half-time performance and received wild applause for his job.

Fragments Without Verbs

Sometimes writers omit the verb, usually because the previous sentence or the next sentence suggests what the verb might be. Compare these fragments with the completed sentences:

Sentence: The speech coach praised the debate team for winning the tournament.

Fragment (no verb):   A real victory for the team and the school.

Corrected (verb added):   It was a real victory for the team and the school.

Corrected (joined to sentence):   The speech coach praised the debate team for winning the tournament, a real victory for the team and the school.

Sentence: Edith shopped for a new winter coat.

Fragment (no verb):   And some insulated boots.

Corrected (verb added):   And she tried on some insulated boots.

Corrected (joined to sentence): Edith shopped for a new winter coat and some insulated boots.

"Baby Sentences"

Perhaps you've written a group of words that has a subject and verb, but you were told it wasn't a sentence. Maybe you wrote something like this:

The football game was a muddy, slippery fiasco.
Because of the rain that fell off and on during all
four quarters.

Both "sentences" seem to express a complete thought,
and each has a subject and a verb:

game was
rain fell

So why is one a good sentence and the other a sentence
fragment? The answer is simple:
 The first is a "parent sentence." It can stand alone and
take care of itself.
 The second is a "baby sentence." It cannot stand alone
or take care of itself. It needs a parent, like this:

The football game was a muddy, slippery fiasco
because of the rain that fell off and on during all
four quarters.

Here's another example:

Sentence: The artist-in-residence works at our
school each week.

Fragment: Drawing caricatures of many of our
students.

Sentence: The artist-in-residence works at our
school each week drawing caricatures
of many of our students.

Let's talk about "parent sentences" and "baby sentences."
If you can understand the difference, you'll be able to
avoid sentence fragments. Here's the explanation:

Some word groups have a subject and verb but cannot stand alone. We'll call them "baby sentences," because they can't stand alone without a parent.

Certain key words start baby sentences. These words start most baby sentences:

after	before	though	who
although	even though	unless	whom
as	if	until	whose
as if	in order that	when	which
as long as	provided that	whenever	that
as much as	since	where	whoever
as soon as	so that	wherever	whomever
as though	than	while	
because			

Here are several examples of baby sentences correctly connected to parent sentences:

Sentence 1:   A thank-you should go to *whoever planted the flowers in the window box.*

Whoever is the subject and *planted* is the verb of the baby sentence. The baby sentence cannot stand alone. It must have a parent sentence.

Sentence 2:   *Because for days Alaskans never see the sun in winter,* depression can be a problem.

Alaskans is the subject and *see* is the verb of the baby sentence. The baby sentence, that starts with the word *because*, cannot stand alone. It must have a parent sentence.

Sentence 3:   The solitary sandpiper earns its name
since it is usually found alone.

It is the subject and *is found* is the verb of the baby sentence. The baby sentence, that starts with the word *since*, cannot stand alone. It must have a parent.

This baby sentence business is really simple if you pay attention to the words that usually start them.

Writing Good Sentences

So what else do you really need to know about good sentences to write and speak well?

Two hints will keep your writing clear and accurate as you write sentences:

1.   Never write a baby sentence as a sentence by itself.

If you capitalize the first word and put a period after the last word of a baby sentence, your reader knows you don't know what a parent sentence is. That's serious. Sentences are the basic component of any writing. Compare these two sentences:

Incorrect: After the tennis match was over on
Saturday morning. (The baby sentence
starts with the word *after* and cannot
stand alone.)

Correct: After the tennis match was over on
Saturday morning, the winners and
losers all shook hands. (The baby
sentence is connected to a parent
sentence.)

2. Use a comma after a baby sentence that starts a sentence. Consider these examples:

Sentence 1: *Whenever Quincy gets a headache,* he just keeps working.

Sentence 2: *Although the politicians say otherwise,* our neighborhood knows the intersection is dangerous.

▶▶▶▶▶▶ COMPOUND SENTENCES ◀◀◀◀◀◀

When we talked about conjunctions (see page 30), we talked about joining two sentences together. When you join two sentences together, the result is called a compound sentence. Here a two reminders about writing good compound sentences:

1. Join two sentences with the correct punctuation.

Use a comma in front of the conjunctions that join two sentences together to make a compound sentence. The conjunctions are

and
but
or
nor
for

Compare these sentences:

Sentence 1	Comma and Conjunction	Sentence 2
Cattails grow readily in marshes	, but	I wanted some growing in my yard pond.
Windstorms whipped through the city	, and	as a result, hundreds of people were without electricity.

2.   Write compound sentences to make your writing and speaking more mature.

You don't want your writing to sound like a first-grader's reading book. You want sophistication. That's achieved by combining lots of short parent clauses into longer baby and parent clauses. Consider these examples:

WEAK PASSAGE:

> Rain pelted the windshield. Drivers couldn't see well. They were approaching an intersection. A pedestrian was rain-soaked. She used her umbrella to shield herself from rain. The umbrella also kept her from seeing. She did not see the cars. They were approaching. She nearly met her demise.

BETTER PASSAGE:

> Because rain pelted the windshield, neither driver could see the approaching intersection well. A rain-soaked pedestrian, her umbrella shielding her from the rain but also obstructing her view of approaching cars, nearly met her demise.

Part 5
Punctuation

There are a whole series of punctuation marks that help readers understand your ideas. The most useful marks include the following:

end marks, like *periods* and *question marks,* that are used at the ends of sentences

commas that show the connections between groups of words

apostrophes and *quotation marks* that have very special uses

How will you ever get all this straight in your mind?

Actually, punctuation is easy if it's boiled down to the basics. And that's what we'll do here.

 **END MARKS**

Every sentence ends with some mark of punctuation. Most sentences end with periods. A sentence that asks a question ends with a question mark.

EXAMPLE: Why didn't we get a newspaper this morning?

With Abbreviations

One end mark is also used for another purpose. Periods are used to mark abbreviations. An abbreviation is a short way of writing something. Consider the following:

names of people: J. L. Smith

titles of people: Mr. Jeffery Smith, Dr. Jane Browne

TIP: *Miss* is not an abbreviation and uses no period. *Ms.,* while it is not really an abbreviation, usually takes a period.

time references: 3:00 P.M., min. (for *minute)*, mo. (for *month*)

geographical locations: S.E. (for *Southeast)*, Third St. (for *Street*), Fla. (for *Florida*)

 **COMMAS**

You'll hear all kinds of advice about using commas. You may even hear someone say to use a comma when you pause. But that, along with other equally vague advice, will get you in trouble on writing tests. It's just as wrong to put commas where they don't belong as it is to leave them out when they do belong. Here are five simple rules that should solve all your problems:

1. Use commas between items in a series.

A series is three or more items listed together. For instance:

	Item 1	Item 2	Item 3
Sentence 1	He	*ate,*	*showered,* and *fell* asleep.
Sentence 2		*Wandell,* *Rodney,*	and *Kathy* cheered for the runners.
Sentence 3	Fierce winds ripped apart	*trees,*	*roofs,*	and *mobile homes.*

TIP: Make items in a series the same kinds of words. For example:

Weak: Jetlyn liked *jogging, hiking,* and *to race* walk.

Better: Jetlyn liked *jogging, hiking,* and *race walking.*

Better: Jetlyn like to *jog, hike,* and *race walk.*

Activity: Think about a sports event you saw recently. Write two sentences about it in which you use a series of items. Be sure to use commas to separate the three or more words in the series.

2. Use a comma with a conjunction that joins two sentences.

We've talked about this before. See explanations and examples on pages 31 and 32.

TIP: Avoid using a comma with a conjunction that joins something other than two sentences. Compare these sentences:

Incorrect: The soccer game included more excitement than usual, and finally ended in a tie after two overtimes.

The comma and conjunction in the sentence above do not join two complete sentences. They join two verbs, *included* and *ended*. Look at it this way:

Part 1		Part 2
The soccer game included more excitement than usual	and	finally ended in a tie after two overtimes.

Part 2 is not a complete sentence. It's a fragment without a subject.

You can correct it one of two ways:

First, you can add a subject and join the two complete sentences with a comma and conjunction:

Correct: The soccer game included more excitement than usual, and it finally ended in a tie after two overtimes.

Or, you can omit the comma:

Correct: The soccer game included more excitement than usual and finally ended in a tie after two overtimes.

Activity: Think about a newspaper article or a television news
show you saw recently. Write a compound sentence about it
using a comma and conjunction to join the two parts. In each
part of the compound sentence, mark the subject with the
letter "s" and the verb with the letter "v" to prove that you have
joined two sentences, not two verbs or two subjects.

3.   Use a comma after a word or group of words that start a sentence.

As you write, you'll find yourself using several kinds of
words and word groups to start a sentence. For the most
part, you can "hear" the comma after an introductory
word or word group. Notice how you can "hear" the comma
in these examples:

> *Norma,* do you think the evaluation was complete?

> *As a result of the evaluation,* Norma earned a pay raise.

4.   Use commas to set off words or word groups that interrupt.

Usually these interrupting words or word groups are easy
to recognize. They're often added to help connect ideas.
For example:

> We expected a victory for Tiger Woods. The victory,
> *however,* was hard-fought. The tournament, *as a
> result,* kept us glued to the television set.

5.   Use commas to set off dates and states.

These examples explain:

> David's birth date is November 9, 1965. (comma to set off
> the year from the day)

David was born in November 1965. (no comma)

David was born in Lexington, Kentucky, in November.
(comma to set off the name of state)

Activity: Think about a movie you've seen recently. Write five
sentences about it, one to illustrate each of the five hints
above about commas. After each sentence, write the
number of the hint your sentence illustrates.

 APOSTROPHES

Apostrophes are used for two reasons:

1. To show ownership

2. To show the missing letter or letters in a contraction

We talked about apostrophes to show ownership when we
talked about nouns on page 5. Here's a quick review:

To make a noun show ownership, add an apostrophe.
If the word does not already end in -*s*, add one after the
apostrophe, like this:

the fox's bushy tail

the foxes' bushy tails

Activity 1: Think about your favorite class. Write a sentence
in which you use the noun *student.* Then write another
sentence in which you use the noun *student's* to show
ownership.

Activity 2: Write a sentence in which you use the plural noun
students. Then write another sentence in which you use the
plural noun *students'* to show ownership.

Use an apostrophe to show the missing letter of letters when you write a contraction, like this:

cannot   = can't
do not   = don't
would not = wouldn't

Activity: Recall a visit to a friend's house. Then write two sentences in which you use contractions. Be sure to use an apostrophe in each contraction to show the missing letter or letters.

 **QUOTATION MARKS**

Occasionally, you may need to use quotation marks. They are used for two primary purposes:

1. To show somebody's exact words

2. To indicate a title

First, we'll look at quotations used to show somebody's exact words. Compare these examples:

EXAMPLE 1:   Paula said, "I don't understand why anyone would want to cut down trees in the park."

Paula's exact words appear inside the quotation marks. Now look at the difference between Example 1 and Example 2.

EXAMPLE 2:   Paula said that she didn't understand why anyone would want to cut down trees in the park.

Do not use quotation marks when you're only telling about what someone said.

Activity: Find a short story in a magazine or literature book. Look for several passages in the story where quotation marks are used. How do the quotation marks help you understand the story?

Quotation marks are also used the mark short titles, like this:

> I read Poe's short story "The Tell-Tale Heart" just before I went to bed and had bad dreams all night.

Activity: Write a sentence in which you name an article or short story you've read recently. Be sure to use quotation marks before and after the title.